I'm Not Broken

You Don't Need Arms to Be Happy

Chet McDoniel

Keller, Texas, USA

To order more,
visit chetmcdoniel.com
or call 817-879-7228.

© 2009 by You Don't Need Arms, LLC
PO Box 77005
Fort Worth, TX 76177
www.chetmcdoniel.com

ISBN 1441428984
EAN-13 9781441428981

Printed in the United States of America.

Dedicated to my dad, without whom, none of these pages would have ever been written.

Preface

On January 5th, 1980, I was born without arms and with shortened legs. Since my birth, my parents have instilled in me a belief that I was no different than anyone else. I was to never let my handicap get in the way of anything I wanted to do. I listened to them, and firmly believe that my life can be as happy as I want it to be regardless of my physical circumstances.

I've had to learn that lesson over 29 years of my life, and as you'll see, I have quite a few things that I've learned. I want to make sure you understand that it wasn't always easy for me to be happy. I've spent many a day when I was in junior high and high school wondering why I look the way I do. I'm not afraid to admit that I have questioned God at those times. I don't think questioning God is something to be ashamed of. We are his children and just as my own kids will one day question some things I do, as long as it is done with respect and with full acknowledgement that He is God and I am not, I believe it can be a healthly way to develop faith.

I have moved passed that stage in my life now. I am fully happy with my life, and as you will see, you can be, too. My life hasn't been without heartache and despair, but by using what I've learned, and what I'm going to share with you, I've gotten by those dark times. I am now able to face anything that comes my way because I know that my attitude determines the happiness in my life. It is under my control, and I choose happiness.

How can I dare to choose happiness when I am so obviously "handicapped?" You'll see...

Contents

1

Define Broken

I have seen the word "broken" defined in many different ways. The word can be used as *physically and forcibly separated into pieces, cracked or split; legally or emotionally destroyed;*

Or *not continuous in space, time, or sequence; varying abruptly;*

Or *lacking a part or parts;*

The last definition strikes a cord with me. Lacking a part or parts...that I am. I was born without arms and my legs are shorter than normal. I use an electric wheelchair to walk long distances, and have many modifications in my home to make life a little easier. So, I meet the definition of broken. But, I am **not** broken.

You see, being broken denotes a need to be fixed. When a car loses a part while driving down the road, and ceases to work, we declare it broken. And, it is broken. If a car will not function, and does not serve its purpose of getting you from point A to point B, then it is by definition, broken. However, what do you do with a broken car? You fix it, or have someone else fix it. You would not let your car sit on the side of the road waiting for it to miraculously start working again, would you? No. You would take it to a knowledgeable person to work on it so that it could again serve you as your mode of transportation. A broken car needs to be fixed.

Take your computer, for example. Everyone hates a broken computer. Not one that is simply slow or does not function properly…I mean a totally non-functioning box. Perhaps the power button on the front is broken, or as those customer service reps in India would have you believe, maybe it just is not plugged in. (Ugh, I promise that's the first thing I checked before I called you…I'm not that absentminded.) When the computer won't power up, or it freezes whenever you open a program, the computer is broken. It does not serve the purpose it was made for and cannot be of any help to you. Again, a broken computer needs to be fixed.

I do not need to be fixed. My life, while far from ordinary, is one in which I **can** serve a purpose. I do not spend time broken down on the side of the road of life waiting for a miraculous event, because I am not in need of such an event. I'm not waiting for my power button to be fixed, because there's no need. While society looks upon me and immediately notices the *lack of parts*, I have never once viewed myself in such a manner. I spend my time living my life to the fullest, and that is exactly what I hope to inspire you to do as well. You can spend your time waiting for your situation to change, or you can get busy living.

Don't You Need a Miracle?

My dad and I were in Tulsa, OK, a few years back at a conference when a woman approached me with a plan. Now, I must tell you that while I am usually the one in the group that is talking, and who wants most to be on stage in the limelight, I am not as well adapted for situations in which complete strangers approach me to strike up a conversation about my handicap. In fact, except for the last year or so of my life, I have been reluctant to talk, write or even contemplate my physical situation. I realized early on in life that if I allowed negative thoughts in, they would typically take up residence. Instead, if I keep those same thoughts at bay, I can focus on the more positive things in my life. So, when this woman approached me (let's call her "Jane"), I was not prepared for the conversation I was about to have.

Jane's son, who was about 40 years old at the time of this story, was walking beside her as she approached us. My dad quickly filled me in on their situation before they came into earshot as he had met them before. Jane's son had been born hydrocephalic at birth, and had a metal plate in his head. He was severally mentally challenged, and she had him tell us "Hello" and state his name. I believed at the time that these were the only two verbalizations he could perform. My heart went out to them, but what she told me next made my stomach turn. She proceeded to tell me that she prayed all-day long, every day for God to perform a miracle, and not only for her son to be medically healed, but that he would also have full cognitive ability as well. She wanted, at the time of the proposed miracle, that he be able to act, think, and behave as if he had been "normal" all along. I had to turn my head away in order to keep my mouth shut. She began to leave as the conversation concluded, but before she left she exclaimed, "Once I get my miracle, I'll start praying for yours." I sat for just a moment and then it hit me…**I don't need her miracle. I don't *want* a miracle.**

This is the most important concept of what I have to tell you, and will be most of what I spend my time on. Now, there are many reasons for this reaction, and I'll go into more details a little later, but I want to give you the foundation and reasoning behind my response. Quite simply, I don't want her miracle because **I'm not broken**. There is nothing about my physical body that I would change at 29 years old.

4

Maybe later, when I'm losing my hair (Who am I kidding? That's happening now!), I'll have something that I would like to be different. For now, though, my lack of arms does not constitute a desire for a miracle. In fact, I've gone so far as to say that I don't understand what "normal" people do with arms. I can write, play video games, drive a car, and type this very book that you are reading all with my feet. Having arms seems superfluous to me because I've never had a use for them. That's what so many people don't understand...there's not a thing wrong with me.

Limitations on God?

Now, I feel the need to express something here to make sure I am not misunderstood. I do believe God is capable of doing whatever He chooses to do. So, if He decided that I should have arms, I believe it would happen. However, while I don't want to get into a theological debate over any of this, I do want to state my opinion that He will never give me arms. Why is that? Simply put, I believe God views my lack of arms the same way I view it. I am not broken, so what is there to fix? If there is nothing wrong with me, and nothing that I want to change about my body, then why would God perform a miracle? He understands, as I do, that there is no

5

"miracle" to be performed. I've never really wanted arms, so I pray for other things…like strength, wisdom, patience, to be a good husband and father…etc.

If you would like to learn more about my family's take on the theology part of the discussion, you'll need to pick up <u>All He Needs for Heaven</u>. (www.allheneedsforheaven.com) My dad and I co-wrote that book, and as he has the doctoral degree, I will defer to him on theology. He does a wonderful job explaining how we all feel about this. God does not cause harm to people.

Who Ya Gonna Call?

I do not believe God caused these deformities, but I do believe He is the one to lean on when times get rough. I've said many times before that God's strength is so immensely more than mine that it sometimes is hard to comprehend. I don't pretend that I haven't had doubts along the way. However, what's amazing about God is that He takes our doubts and allows us to grow stronger. Where a human would be offended if you doubted him/her, God simply shows that He is stronger than our doubts, and allows us to beat on His chest while we learn a deeper understanding of Him. Sure, I've had doubts, but I also know who I can and will turn to in those times. God is my strength and my refuge and in Him, every unwhole thing is made whole, again.

If I'm Not Broken, Then Neither Are You

With that out of the way, I want to explore some areas of my life for you so that you can catch a glimpse of why I believe that every person can live their own life to the fullest, no matter the situation that life's circumstances has placed them in. Your life and how you live it, is totally and completely determined by your attitude and perception. As I have said before, if I can choose happiness, so can you. While you may have arms, there is still some part of your life that you possibly consider broken. I'm here to tell you...you are not broken...and neither am I.

Who is Broken?

You know what annoys me? People who *think* they aren't worth anything.

I had a friend in high school that frustrated me to no end. She was in choir with me and she was a drop-dead knockout. She had a beautiful voice, she was intelligent, and she had tons of friends. She had more going for her than many other students at our high school. Except...she didn't believe in herself.

One time, I was helping out for a choral show as one of the stage managers. My friend was up on stage singing her solo during a rehearsal when her knees started to wobble, and she collapsed to the ground. This would have been scary enough, but she was also on a runway over the orchestra pit, so the ground she collapsed to was only about 3 feet wide. After we got over the initial shock, we discovered that she was okay, but disoriented. We got her down off the stage, and my furious choir director ordered me to get to the bottom of the matter. I started talking to my friend to try and uncover the truth only to find out that she hadn't eaten...

All day...

Now, if you take one look at me, you'll know that I don't miss a meal. I couldn't imagine why a high school student would starve herself all day. I took her aside, got her a sandwich, and dug a little deeper. At first, she was very reluctant to tell me what was going on, but as I probed deeper, I found the truth. She was so nervous that she couldn't eat.

Nervous about the rehearsal...**no.**
Nervous about the show coming up...**no.**
Nervous about the test tomorrow in history class...**no.**

She was nervous because she believed that she would fail those authority figures who trusted in her. **She had so little self-confidence, that she chose to harm herself by not eating instead of realizing the truth.** She could accomplish whatever she set her mind to...and she did, time after time, but it was something that she never taught herself to believe in. She regained her strength and rejoined the cast to continue through the rehearsal.

I was disturbed by this, though, and it continued with me. **Why would people choose not to believe in themselves?** I completely understand not believing in someone who has let you down before. We build trust in other people because, in a sense, others have to earn our true trust. But, with self-trust, it should be automatic, right? As I grew older, and saw more of the world around me, I realized...it wasn't automatic. Self-trust has to be taught.

That Third Child Who Won't Let Anyone Tell Him, "No"

When I was young, I began to grow a passion for worship leading. My dad taught a fourth, fifth and sixth grade boys' leadership class on Sunday afternoons. He would work with us boys on how to lead singing, how to lead prayer, and how to preach so that we would be able to develop God given skills in worship service leadership. Once a quarter, we would lead an entire Sunday evening service. I excelled at song leading. My voice is a gift from God, and I thank Him for that. He put a passion in my heart for exciting, exuberant worship, and to this day, that's why I love leading worship.

I used my talent in worship leading off and on growing up, and then in the summer of 2005, I decided that I wanted to pursue a full-time career as a worship minister. After spending many nights in prayer, and discussing all of our options with my wife, we decided to pursue this calling by sending out resumes. I called and told my dad (who, to this day I share almost everything with), and he was excited. He and I shared all of the possibilities, and concluded the conversation.

Now, throughout my life, my mother has needed "delicate handling" when it comes to things happening in my life. She overflows with love and concern for me, and sometimes, my decisions shock her into defensive mode. I even remember one time in which she thought my dad was performing a cruel action towards me by taking me to a Six Flags job fair. I got the job, and told her that the cruel thing to do would have been to tell me, "no." I wasn't always as gentle as I should have been. Her desire to protect me still extends to this day. Isn't that the mark of a good mother?

Dad realized after our conversation about being a worship minister that he would have to "break the news" to mom. So, when my mom got home from school that night, my dad said... "Well...you know that 3rd child we have...you know...the one who won't let anyone tell him 'No!'" She smiled as she knew something was coming. He then told her my desire to become a worship minister. And, I did lead worship for just over a year at the Plymouth Park Church of Christ in Irving, TX. I chose to leave that position in order to pursue a speaking career, but I still lead worship for other events. Leading worship will always remain a passion.

I LOVE being described as someone who won't let anyone tell me, "No." Maybe I sound obstinate or stubborn, which I am, but I take it as a compliment. My whole life, people have tried to tell me what I can and can't do. From doctors, to friends, to people whom I didn't even know, I've always had people explaining my limitations to me.

Before our daughter, Hannah, was born, people started giving me advice. Most of the advice was simply about parenthood, however many people who did not know us very well insisted that some adjustments be made so that I could cuddle with Hannah once she was born. The folks giving this advice were

well meaning, but I must say that their advice bothered me. See, I will never hold Hannah like everyone else. But, for me, this is not a sad thing. I just have to learn "what works for me" in each and every situation. So when I hold Hannah, she's not against my chest, but then again, how else would I feel her without being able to touch her with my feet? My feet are my hands.

I was given more advice to make sure and buy a sling to put her in so that she could be up against my chest. We bought one…but we won't use it. If we put her in the sling, I would inevitably want her out and on my lap or on the floor so that I can bond with, play with, and touch my daughter. It may not look like how you would bond with your child…it may not look like how my own wife bonds with Hannah…but it is **what works for me!**

I know my limitations; I live in this body everyday. No one can tell me I can't do something. No one can tell me, "No." (Well, unless it's my wife, Joni…then I'll listen.)

Who's Due Congratulations for My Stubbornness?

From day one, my parents tried to teach me that I was no different than anyone else. If the kids at school were participating in an activity, I was in the middle of it. If friends were doing something dumb and dangerous, I was usually in the middle of it. In fact, I even played a game of "Alcho-Ball" with my high school friends on my back porch.

"Alcho-Ball" is a game in which you take a tennis ball that has been soaking overnight in rubbing alcohol, and you play hot-potato with it…

While it is on fire…

See, a friend of mine learned in chemistry class that alcohol burns at a relatively cool temperature, and if you catch the lit tennis ball and throw it all in one motion, you don't get

13

burned. "Alcho-Ball" is especially fun to play in the dark. Okay, okay, so that was a horribly dumb thing for us to do. And, as they say on MythBusters (TV show on Discovery Channel), "Don't try anything you see us do...EVER." Well, same warning applies.

Do you see my point, though? I never knew that I was different. Oh, I wasn't under the illusion that I looked like everyone else, but just because I don't look the same, doesn't mean I have to act differently. My parents wanted a child who lived a normal life, and they got it; the good and the bad.

Brokenness is Obvious

I can spend only a few moments in conversation with someone and tell you whether I believe them to be broken or not. Brokenness, represented by a lack of self-esteem, shows up in almost every thing a broken person does. From the self-deprecating speech patterns, to a lack of willingness to take risks. **A broken person lives a broken life.** And while they may not realize it, their life is not set in stone. The way you act and talk today does not necessarily dictate the way you act and talk tomorrow.

When a person is living a broken life, they bring everyone else down around them. Often, in my presentations to businesses, schools, churches and other groups, I talk about the negative person that everyone knows. I tell people that everyone has a negative friend. You can picture that person now. They always gripe at work about how bad their day has been. Maybe they are the school friend who complains constantly about mean teachers and workload.

Do you like being around those people?
Do you seek them out to listen to their gripes?
Do you not try to run the other direction when you see them coming?

NO ONE likes to be around negative people. (Unless you, yourself are negative, and if you are…listen up!) Life is hard enough by itself, but when you are around someone who has a hard time seeing positive things around them, it makes life unbearable.

The person that is griping all the time or can't say anything good about their day IS BROKEN. No two ways about it, if negativity is all that comes out of someone, they have a broken personality. I don't use broken as a label or a way to call names, but rather, I use it as a strong term to call attention to how many Americans live. And the sad thing is…they don't have to live that way.

You see, being broken is a horrible way to live. But, it is also an easy way to live.

Addicted to Being Broken

Remember my friend from choir in high school? She went right back to her lack of self-confidence as soon as she came out of her dizzy spell. She learned nothing from the situation. She could easily have fallen off of the runway into the orchestra pit, and I wouldn't have been forcing her to eat...I would have been calling 911. The stage crew even had to develop a routine to ask her if she had eaten before a rehearsal or show. That's where I learned to always have a Power Bar on me when I was managing a show.

You see, my friend didn't have an eating problem. She had an addiction to being broken. She had an addiction to a low self-esteem. And, why not? I mean, until you realize that your lack of self-esteem hurts not only yourself, but those around you, why bother changing? Change is difficult, and quite frankly, when you have a low self-esteem, people expect less of you. When people expect less of you, you can expect less of yourself. The cycle keeps continuing until YOU do something to break it.

Experts say that many behavioral addictions are just as strong as chemical addictions. Alcoholics don't develop a chemical need for alcohol, rather, a condition forms in the brain in which being drunk removes life's problems...and those endorphins are stronger than most chemicals. Some who are addicted to pornography have a very hard time breaking away

16

from the endorphin rush that comes when looking at naked pictures.

People who have low self-esteem are addicted to this behavior. They get their self-worth from tearing other people down. They get it from making sure you know how bad of a day they've had. Anything they can do to make you feel worse, makes them feel better. They don't believe in themselves, so they need you to stop believing in yourself in order to make them feel better. They are **addicted** to needing to feel better about themselves. We all like feeling good about ourselves, but a "whole" people have many different ways that they can feel good about themselves. Those things are much of what we are going to discuss in later chapters. But, someone who has low self-esteem cannot come up with any other way to feel better, because they don't believe in themselves first.

Brokenness is Not Incurable

What's so incredible about our minds is not how fast we can think or how much information we can store...but rather, we have the opportunity to change our minds whenever we **want** to. We have the power to change our actions, behaviors, and even our speech. We can change. You can change.

Let me break off for a moment to address depression. Clinical depression is **NOT** what I am addressing when I say "broken." Depression is very real, and is often caused by a chemical imbalance in the brain. I highly recommend seeking professional medical attention if you can't work yourself out of depression. Modern medicine is a gift from God. Take advantage of it. Just as people with low self-esteem have the power to change, so do you. Call your medical professional and get help.

Now, with that out of the way, I want to give you the great news that a grumpy attitude is not incurable. In fact, there are simple ways that you can implement to make the change. These changes are so easy that you can start making them when the alarm clock goes off, tomorrow.

Remember my collapsing friend? Well, chances are you've seen her on primetime television in one or more major TV shows. She obviously broke herself of her negative habits. Either that, or she drives the crew crazy with fainting spells.

You see, you have to want to change. Some people don't want to make their lives better. What about them? I say, they can't continue to live that way. God has no intention for his creation to live with negative attitudes. How do I know that? In John 10:10, Jesus says:

> "The thief cometh not, but for to steal, and to kill, and to destroy: I am come that they might have life, and that they might have it **more abundantly**."

18

The Wrong Side of the Bed

In my talks and presentations I always share that there are two sides of the bed I can choose to wake up from every morning...the right side, full of a bright happy life and the wrong side, which is non-stop whining, complaining, and negativity. I see so many people choosing the wrong side every day. What amazes me is that those who choose the wrong side do not understand that they are missing out on what it means to live life, **more abundantly**.

Cork-screw Ambition

When I was in my junior year in high school, I was hired to work in Operations at Six Flags Over Texas. Being a huge theme park fan, I loved the job, and it was a great way to pass the summer. When I first started there I was just a regular ride operator, but within a few months I was promoted to Assistant Supervisor, and then all the way to Ride Supervisor. My rise from an entry-level position to a supervisor was one of the shortest spans my Area Manager had ever seen. I inquired into why that was…

Was I that good?
Was I that smart?
Was I that equipped to be a supervisor?

She surprised me with her answer. She said I was one of the only park employees that seemed to want to advance. **What?** You mean all of these other employees were content in entry-level positions? Did they have no drive, no ambition? "Precisely" she answered.

Brokenness is Comfortable

Have you ever thought about the janitor that works in your office building, or the clerk in the mail room? Did they once dream about a better career? When they were children, did they really answer the "What do you want to be when you grow up?" question: "Janitor?" or "Entry-level worker?" Now, maybe they've found purpose in their jobs, and feel fulfilled. If that is the case, then they should be proud of what they've accomplished. They should also share their secrets on how to find purpose in everyday life. But, for those who are in those jobs because they have no ambition, I challenge that they are comfortable with living a broken life.

I saw a commercial on TV years ago that I believe was for a job/career service. The commercial featured children in grade school telling the camera that they wanted to be "Yes" men when they grew up. They kept saying over and over that they wanted to be middle management...just follow the boss's orders. The commercial came to a conclusion as the narrator announced "No one wants to be a 'Yes' man...find your dream job, now." I thought it was very funny because of the ridiculous nature of the kids' answers. No one dreams of a dead-end job or a dead-end life. But, the sad fact is that so many people get locked into jobs and lives they don't like because having a lack of self-confidence is so comfortable.

As humans, we resist change. Our surroundings make us comfortable, and we resist all change whether it is good or bad. This was easily seen at Six Flags. So many teenagers at the Park did not have any ambition to go any higher than entry-level. Okay...maybe I just took a summer job a little too seriously. But, that's how I approach life. If you don't take risks, and you don't have ambition, you'll always be in the same rut as you are today. Maybe that is a comfortable place to be, but is it a happy place to be?

Brokenness is Unhappiness

When you choose the wrong side of the bed every day, it can wear you down. A negative self-image partnered with a lack of ambition leads to a broken life. The spiral continues downward until you decide that you can't be happy, unless:

You have more money...
Or more security...
Or better health...

A 2003 World Value Survey of people in 65 nations was published in the British magazine, *New Scientist*. The survey found that the world's happiest countries with the most satisfied people are Puerto Rico and Mexico, and those with the most optimistic people are Nigeria and Mexico.

The United States? A dismal 16th place.

Does More Money = Happiness?

Let's first consider material wealth as measured by each nation's Gross Domestic Product (GDP) per capita: 2003 estimates showed the US with a GDP per person of $37,800. But, we're only in 16th place...surely the happier countries make more than we do!

22

Well, what about the happiest nations? GDP per person in Puerto Rico is $16,800; in Mexico it is $9,000; in Nigeria it is a pitiful $800.

Obviously money has **very little** to do with happiness.

Does Peace/Security = Happiness?

Though set on a lush island paradise, the US territory of Puerto Rico suffers a high murder rate and double-digit unemployment. Materially among the world's poorest people, Nigerians also have to contend with living in one of the world's most corrupt countries, where government services and infrastructure has largely broken down or are unreliable, violence is rife and human life is cheap.

So, safety/peace doesn't necessarily lead to happiness.

Does Education and Health = Happiness?

In the 2003 United Nations Human Development Indicators ranking, Nigeria was 152nd out of 175 countries, or 24th from the bottom for life expectancy, health, education, standard of living, and literacy.

So, true happiness is not about prosperity, peace, education, health or even life expectancy.

What Equals Happiness, Then?

The study found two indicators of the happiest nations. They had a strong sense of community, and they had frequent, enthusiastic community celebrations. They are enjoying life through each other. Happiness equals a positive attitude and learning to be happy when someone else is happy.

As noted over a century ago by Emile Durkheim, the French founder of modern sociology, "adversity itself encourages the formation of societal relationships and can actually promote positive feelings."

When we learn to get through our differences, and to be happy for our fellow man, WE become happy. What a concept! One of the areas we will focus on later is getting involved in the community as a way of preventing a broken attitude.

Focusing on someone else instead of yourself is a great way to start your journey towards a happy life. But what about those who continually put others down?

It All Comes Down to a Snoodle

Our 10 month old has become enthralled with Bob and Larry from VeggieTales. Joni and I think VeggieTales is much better than much of the kids' programming currently running on television, so we are glad she is so taken by the tomato and

cucumber. There is one episode in particular that was re-
corded on our DVR and has been played over and over again
in our living room. I love the message in the story, as it
teaches self-worth in a way that we all need to learn.

In the episode, "A Snoodle's Tale," Bob the Tomato tells a
Dr. Seuss-like story of a little creature known as a Snoodle.
Now, most Snoodles are of average size, however, the young
Snoodle playing the main role in the story is smaller than the
others. He tries his hand at art, music and even flying, but his
talents are not as developed as the other Snoodles in town.
The Snoodles around him ridicule his efforts and make him
feel terrible for even trying. Every time the young Snoodle
fails at something, the other Snoodles paint him a picture to
commemorate the failure, and they place each painting in his
backpack. He eventually decides to leave town and head toward Mt. Ginches where he has seen the local "finches"
flying and soaring through the sky.

Once he reaches the top of Mt. Ginches, he finds a cave
which is located "high above the clouds." Inside the cave, we
meet a Stranger, the Creator of the Snoodles (which is a rep-
resentation of God himself). The Stranger sees the young
Snoodle is very depressed, and he asks to see the paintings in
his backpack. The young Snoodle reluctantly complies, and is
surprised when the Stranger announces that these paintings
look nothing like the young Snoodle. The Stranger tosses the
terrible memories of the failures into the fire, and tells the
Snoodle that He will paint a true image for him to carry in his

pack. Here are the words from the poem as it is told just as the Stranger has revealed His painting of the young Snoodle:

The boy in the portrait looked older and strong,
With wings on his back that were sturdy and long,
And a look in his eye, both courageous and free.
"Sir," asked the boy, "Are you saying that's—me?
I'd like to believe it, but, sir, I'm afraid to."
"I know who you are," the man said, "for I made you.

"I've seen you fall down in the mud and the goo.
I've seen all you've done and all you will do.
I gave you your pack and your paints and your wings.
I chose them for you. They're your special things."

"The Snoodle-kazoo is so you can sing
About colors in autumn or flowers in spring.
I gave you your brushes in hopes that you'd see
How using them, you can make pictures for me."
"Most of the Snoodles," the old one said sadly,
"Just use their paints to make others feel badly."

In the story, the Stranger (God) tells us that most Snoodles "just use their paints to make others feel badly." **That's the wrong side of the bed.** Using what you have, your talents (even if you don't believe you have any), and/or your attitude to bring down others so that you can feel better.

Don't you see? You've been given so much more than that. You've been given life, breath, and a family; maybe you've even been given arms. If you have, you've been given more than I have in the sense of a whole body.

You have the power to choose the right side of the bed. You have the power to change your life to be a happy one. It is time to get out of our comfort zones, and choose to take a chance on a happy life. I guarantee you; you won't go back once you've discovered life, **more abundantly.**

But, how do we get there?

Smile As if the World Depends on it…

Because it Does

We Americans are an unhappy breed. We have already established in the previous chapter that we are not the highest rated country on the happiness list. So, what's the problem? Why do we live in a society that is so broken? I have a few answers that come from my own observations, and I'm going to cover them over the next several chapters. The first answer for you is that we are unhappy because we don't smile enough.

We've spent years getting away from each others' lives. What were once small fences to show property lines are now full wooden fences blocking the view of nosy neighbors. We live on the Internet, a place where anonymity is a prized possession. My wife and I won't even answer our front door unless we know the person standing on the other side (or they are in a UPS/FedEx uniform). We value our privacy. And, to a degree, I believe we should value it. I have yet to understand reality TV shows. Not from the perspective of the viewer…I completely understand why Americans are fascinated with other people's lives. I don't understand, though, why these contestants would chose to exchange their privacy for a little fame or a little money. Some things in life are sacred.

In his book, <u>Sex God</u>, Rob Bell talks about things that should be only between husband and wife, especially in terms of their sex lives. He says that some things are ruined when others are involved. Not just with an affair, but even telling someone outside the relationship all the juicy details can permanently damage a husband and wife's intimacy.

But, in a world so governed by less and less human contact, should we be completely separated from all human interaction?

Wouldn't a Phone Call Be Easier?

My dad and I were driving in a rental car from the Fresno, California airport to the town of Visalia where we were to present our "All He Needs" presentation at the Tulare-Kings Right-to-Life organization. I had promised to call my wife when we had landed and were on our way because she was back at home with Hannah. I picked up the phone and proceeded to text her that we were safe and on the way to the banquet. My dad asked, "Why would you text? What's the advantage there? Wouldn't a phone call be easier?"

Now, I think it was a genuine question as his tone sounded to me like he was asking about the technology more than trying to get me to think. But, it did make me think. Why was I texting? Just because it is what everyone else does? But I'm not everyone else. So, I picked up the phone again, and called my wife. We had a wonderful conversation. It felt great to hear her voice, and to hear about her day with Hannah. I could hear her smiling on the other end. Smiles can lift your day like nothing else.

Smile For No Reason

Did you know that there are over 50 types of identified smiles? Think about it. You can use different smiles to show that you are happy, excited, polite, inviting, and you can even use a smile to show fear and/or contempt. We are very good at twisting simple actions to mean exactly what we are feeling. In fact, my wife and I know when something is wrong by the way the other smiles. My wife has smiles of joy, and smiles that mean I should inquire as to what is going on. I have them, too.

Sometimes smiling has nothing to do with underlying thoughts and emotions. People smile because it is what is expected of them. Think about the salesman who wants you to buy from him, or the politician who wants your vote. Are they smiling to make you feel better? Well, in a way, yes, but they have motives underneath their smiles. They aren't smiling just to make you feel better...they're smiling to get something from you.

What I'm suggesting here as a way to combat unhappiness is to **smile for no reason**. Put aside ulterior motives of trying to get a favor from someone, or trying to get something for nothing and just **smile**. Your smile can literally change someone's day. Remember the whining co-worker we talked about? What if you could change his/her day just by listening to their problem, smiling, and telling them you are here for them. Wow. Think about what that would mean for you. Even if you don't have a chance to talk to them on a given day after that conversation, they'll know your smile means you have taken an interest in their life, and that you will support them in whatever way is needed.

Smile to Make Someone Else Feel Better

Years ago, I was on a cruise with my extended family. We were having a wonderful time, and everything was going well. Then, out of nowhere, one of our table mates chewed out our table server because the food she had received was undercooked. The table mate really let the server have it, and completely caused an unnecessary scene. The server, with a very quiet voice, explained that she would be glad to fix the issue. She picked up the food, and left the table. As you can guess, the conversation at the table stalled out and the meal quickly became uncomfortable even after the food issue was corrected.

My dad, my mom, and I noticed something, though, that we decided to see if we could fix. The table server would not make eye contact with anyone at our table for the rest of the meal, and she appeared to tear up any time she was spoken to. We decided that for the rest of the cruise, our job was to make her feel better. For every other meal we had, we tried to treat the server with respect and smiles. By the end of the cruise, we had made a new friend. The server would seek us out while walking about the ship if she saw us, and she did everything she could to make sure we were having a great time. We changed her day...maybe even her week because we made sure to make her feel good every chance we got. I'm not even sure the rude table mate was aware of the situation after she made her outburst, but I guarantee you the evening meal time went much better once we started to get to know the server.

I have a friend named David who tips more for poor service at restaurants than he does for good service. "How ridiculous," most people would say. We tip based on how well they performed their job. David says that he thinks we should stop for a moment and put ourselves in the poor server's shoes. What if they are having a bad day? What if the manager yelled at them earlier? What if they don't feel good? And then, the question that changed my attitude about poor service... "Would I want rude customers and horrible tips to compound a bad day?" Amazing! David said that he simply smiles, tips big, and hopes that his attitude and generosity brightens their day.

Smile...Your Job Could Depend On It

In 2007, I had the privilege to hear a man by the name of Tim Sanders speak at a Disney convention for travel agents. (In addition to speaking and writing, I own a travel agency – Off to Neverland Travel – www.offtoneverland.com)

Tim used to be an executive at Yahoo! and he told us how they used to screen job applicants to find the right person for an open position.

When an applicant would come in for the scheduled interview, he/she was given a secret test upon greeting the receptionist. If that test was failed, no matter how well the subsequent interview went, no matter how great the applicant's references were, and no matter what experience the applicant had, he/she would NOT be hired. If the simple, secret test did not go well, the applicant could do nothing to salvage the interview. Ok...ready for what the test was?

The applicant was tested on whether or not he/she would smile at the receptionist.

And that smile would determine the applicant's future with the company. What??? A smile??? Sanders went on to say that Yahoo! felt it could teach and train anyone for the job, but they couldn't train personality. They had found that a team that worked well together with positive personalities got more work done than the most qualified people in the world. A smile could land you a job!

Smile...Your Health May Depend On It

In an article on About.com entitled, "What's in a Smile?," writer Kimberly Read says, "In psychology, there is a theory entitled the 'facial feedback' hypothesis. This hypothesis states that 'involuntary facial movements provide sufficient peripheral information to drive emotional experience' (Bernstein, et al., 2000). Davis and Palladino explain that 'feedback from facial expression affects emotional expression and behavior' (2000). In simple terms, you may actually be able to improve your mood by simply smiling!"

Let's face it though, sometimes, we don't feel like smiling. Well, I've got a solution for you, and maybe you've heard it before. **Act your way into a good mood.** In other words, research has shown that when we don't feel happy, one of the best things we can do is to act like we do feel happy. Smiling, laughing, and doing other things that we do when we are in a good mood can actually help us to get in a better mood. Try it the next time you are in a bad mood. Smile until your face muscles hurt, or until you are out of your funk…whichever comes first.

10 Smiles Per Hour Zone

Did you know that in Australia, where being open and friendly to strangers is not unusual, the city of Port Phillip has been using volunteers to find out how often people smile at those who pass them in the street? It then put up signs that look like speed limits, but tell pedestrians that they are in, for example, a "10 Smiles Per Hour Zone."

Writer Peter Singer (in his article "No Smile Limit") says, "Frivolous nonsense? A waste of taxpayers' money? Mayor Janet Bolitho says that putting up the signs is an attempt to encourage people to smile or say "G'day"—the standard Australian greeting—to both neighbors and strangers as they stroll down the street. Smiling, she adds, encourages people to feel more connected with each other and safer, so it reduces fear of crime—an important element in the quality of life of many neighborhoods."

So, could your neighborhood street be a 10 Smiles Per Hour Zone? Only if you choose to make it one…

The Smile Experiment

One of my presentations, "The Smile Experiment" ends with a challenge that I am going to give you now. Tomorrow, I want you to commit to smiling all day long. That means from the moment the alarm clock rings until the moment your head hits the pillow for the night, I challenge you to smile. The first thing you'll notice is that your face will hurt because we don't exercise those muscles enough. But beyond that, I guarantee you that you will have a better day than you did today. You'll brighten the days of those around you, and in turn, those to whom you smile will likely pass on that smile to others.

I usually challenge entire schools to participate and I tell the teachers and administrators that they must participate, too. Get your whole department, office, or company participating in The Smile Experiment! Read what one teacher had to say about the experiment:

"Thanks so much for blessing me and for blessing our students with your positive message of self-accountability. Smile Day continues here at Dawson!"

Continues? It wasn't just one day? That's right, because once you experience the power of a smile, you'll choose to smile everyday!

Change Your Perspective:
Shoes or No Shoes?

One of my favorite illustrations to use when speaking proposes the story of two shoe salesmen. They are each from separate companies, and are flown in to a remote location in Africa. They both come upon a tribe that has never even seen shoes before let alone have ever worn them.

The first salesman arrives, sees the lack of shoes, and immediately calls back to his company's headquarters. "Stop the order," he exclaims, "No one here wears shoes. There's no chance for a sale."

The second salesman arrives, sees the lack of shoes, and also, immediately calls back to his company's headquarters.

"Triple the order," he exclaims, "No one here wears shoes. I can sell a pair to every tribe member."

Same Situation, Different Perspective

How many times have you approached a situation only to see the negative? For a very real reason, my parents could initially only see heartbreak and devastation when I was born. In our "All He Needs" presentation, my dad talks about the hopelessness they felt when they first saw me. He says that many nights, he and my mom would stand over my crib with tears in their eyes because they could not see a future for a child with no arms. Had they been able to see how life turned out for me, I doubt they would have had any sadness. But, hindsight's 20/20, right?

Sometimes, our past failures can lock our perspective into a negative viewing lens. If you've failed in the past at achieving your dreams, then you may view your dreams as unattainable. You have to get out of that frame of mind. Walt Disney is quoted as saying, "If we can dream it, we can do it." I believe him!

When I decided to become a worship minister, I was full of ambition and motivation. I sent out resumes to every church where I thought my style would fit in. I was interviewed by many of them, but once I would bring up my handicap, the tone of the interview would change, and I usually didn't hear back.

After more than a few times of being rejected, my quest became discouraging. I decided, though, to keep pressing on, and kept sending out resumes. A small church in Irving, TX brought me in to interview. I tried out on the following Sunday by leading worship for the morning, and was hired on the spot. Success!

Why did I keep going? Why did I not allow the discouragement to stop me from achieving my goal? Simple. **I believed that I could do it.** I believed that becoming a worship minister was an attainable goal, and I kept seeing the situation with a positive attitude. I knew that if I kept pursuing a position, eventually my skill-set and personality would match with what a church was looking for. **I never once considered that I wouldn't be able to get the job.** It never entered my mind. I knew I was more than capable, and someone would see that.

I loved my worship ministry time at the Plymouth Park Church of Christ, and they were wonderful to me. I would have never had the opportunity to lead and to learn at that church had I not kept a positive attitude during my job search. If I hadn't seen the silver lining while seeking the position, I would have missed out on a valuable experience in my life.

You Want Me to Talk to...7th Graders???

In March of 2007, my dad and I were approached by a teacher at Dawson Middle School in Southlake, TX to come and speak to their 7th grade class. They were reading the book, <u>The Acorn People</u>, which deals with a camp for kids with special needs. The book has a great sense of humor, and this teacher had heard about our story. She believed it would be great to have the students hear from someone who had special needs, but who also had a happy attitude. However the kicker was that she thought it would be best for the students to have a Q & A time with me after the presentations.

YIKES!

I wasn't so sure about this. I mean, it is one thing to speak to a church crowd of mostly adults. We were used to that. Church people make a great audience as they have already been trained to listen during worship service, and we can always get them laughing while inspiring at the same time. But teenagers? And, particularly middle school teenagers? I feared going in to speak that morning as I knew they could be a tough crowd. I also feared their questions. What if a question was asked that was too personal? How would I handle it?

Still, being able to see the positive in the situation (the paycheck), I accepted the "gig." I tell you now, as I tell every school, **7th graders are my FAVORITE crowd.** Not only were they respectful, I learned that they still have the optimism that so many adults let go of years ago. One might say that their optimism is naïve because of a lack of life experiences. I say, "Bologna!" **They are optimistic because they choose to be.** You should have heard some of their questions:

> **"What would you consider to be your biggest triumph in life?"**

> **"If you could say one thing to lift someone's day, what would it be?"**

> **"Name one person who inspired you in life, and how you can take what that person did and inspire others."**

WOW! Not only were they thinking deep, but they wanted to know how to better the lives of the people around them. They wanted to know how to make their school a better place by inspiring others to live in a positive community. The experience was amazing, and few other times have I come away with such an adrenaline high. These kids have it. They know how to make the world a better place. And, they are OUR future. I'd say the future is in good hands, and I look forward to the invitation to return to that school (and invitations to any other school) that I've gotten since.

I Don't Have Arms. So, What?

The obvious thing here is to spend some time on what it means to be able to see the positive side of not having arms. Upon first glance, many people see me as un-whole, handicapped, and typically take pity on me. Why? Because they don't know the awesome life I live. I don't have arms…

…But I can drive a van that has special equipment.

…But I can type with my feet at over 35 words per minute

…But I can write with my feet

…But I can feed myself and brush my teeth with my feet

…But I can "hold hands" with my wife…with my feet

…But I can hold my daughter up in the air and play "Super Hannah" with my feet

Yes, there are elements to not having arms that genuinely "bite it." I have daily aches and pains that won't ever go away because my body is not designed to do the things I do

43

with it. For instance, some doctors told my parents early on that I wouldn't be able to walk. I can walk just fine; however, long distances are a problem due to having no bone support structure in my hips. I walk on sheer muscle mass and will-power. I can't do some things for myself that others take for granted. There are problems in life. **But...you don't need to be missing limbs to know that, right?**

Instead, focusing on the positive has allowed me to develop a personality that my wife found attractive enough to want to marry me. I have a great career spreading joy to as many people as I can through books and presentations. I have a daughter, who just after learning to crawl, finds her favorite spot curled up in my lap. (I know that won't last forever, but I'm loving it while it does.) All of these things in my life would have never happened had it not been for my passion and zest for a happy life.

How did I get here? **You have to decide to see the positive lining in EVERY situation.** No matter what occurs, there is always something good that can come from it. Hey, I may not have arms...but my story got you to listen...there's one positive! ☺

Don't Whine

My dad has said many times that he believes one thing worse than having a handicapped child would be to have one that complains all of the time. I love it! Nothing gets on my nerves faster than someone who whines. Whining accomplishes nothing other than getting the listener to feel sorry for you. Why would you want their pity? I certainly don't!

It is All in the Attitude

Before I went to the University of North Texas, I spent two years at Tarrant County College in order to stay at home and get my basic courses out of the way. There was a disability advocate group on campus that tried to recruit me while I was there. At first, I was interested in the group, but upon inquiring their overall goal, I quickly made myself unavailable.

I was told that the group's goal was to demand their rights and make the school listen to their demands. I told the recruiter that it sounded like a "gripe-fest" to me and that those types of events serve no purpose.

You see, I believe that getting your rights (what's really due to you out of fairness and kindness) is all in your attitude when it comes to your complaint. I own a travel agency (OfftoNeverland.com), and have received many phone calls over the years from people who needed something from me. Let's take a look the following two scenarios that really did happen:

Scenario 1:
Ring...Ring...

"Off to Neverland Travel, this is Chet."

"Chet, this is (name of client) I can't believe you let that cruise line route my airfare through Chicago when I told you I didn't want that."

"Ma'am, I did pass that information on to the cruise line, and I told you at that time, if you wanted to have a special air itinerary set up, you'd have to pay an air deviation fee. You told me you didn't think it was worth it."

"Well, now I do, I DEMAND you re-route the flight."
"It isn't that easy. At this point, the cruise line has already set up your itinerary, and they'll charge you a change fee plus the difference in cost of your preferred itinerary."

"WHAT??? I can't believe this. You are so incompetent. I will never use this agency, again."

Click. (At the end of this call, I was thinking that I was glad this rude client was never going to call again. Less stress for me!)

Scenario 2:
Ring...Ring...

"Off to Neverland Travel, this is Chet."

"Hi Chet. This is (name of client), and I was calling because we would love to see if we can get a different cabin on the ship. We're not too fond of the one we're currently booked in."

"Hi, well, the problem is that we are really close to the sail date, and the ship is quite full."

"Well, if it can't be done, then we understand. After all, you did send us our paperwork months ago, and we are

just now wanting to change. It's our fault, but is there anything you can do?"

"I will be more than happy to do my best in order to get you what you want…"

Did you see the difference? In Scenario 1, the client was whiny and flat-out rude when she pointed the fault at me even though it was not mine to begin with. I was not inclined to help her out, especially after she hung up on me. (By the way, I was able to get her airfare changed and negotiated a really low fee on the whole thing which I paid for. Was she happy with that? Yes, but she still never called again. That's okay, I didn't want her as a client anymore.)

The caller in Scenario 2 had a completely different tone throughout the conversation. Again, the situation was her fault, but she acknowledged it and simply asked me if there was anything I could do. I was able to get them a better stateroom, and I even threw in a surprise gift for them that they found when arriving at their cabin. I wanted to help them because they were nice to me.

The difference? Whining. Demanding. Playing the blame game. I am convinced that you can get so much farther in life when you approach these types of situations with a smile. In fact, I regularly place the blame on myself when I call a company to complain. You would be amazed at how refreshing that is for the customer service representative, and how often I get my way.

We Aren't Owed Anything

My parents taught me at a young age that I was no different from anyone else. I wasn't owed anything, nor did the world have to bend over backwards to make me happy. I am grateful for that early lesson, and it was even shown to me in high school.

I had a wheelchair in high school that would short out whenever it rained. The slightest bit of water on the control stick and the chair would go dead. One day I was on my way to class when I was stopped, dead in my tracks. I called my dad who was always my rescuer, and he came out to take the control stick apart in order to dry it. Before he could, he had to push me to my next class. Most people don't realize that if your electric wheelchair stops working, you can't go anywhere. Imagine if your legs just froze and wouldn't move. It's debilitating.

My high school had the look of a community college with all of the different buildings separated and spread apart. My dad arrived and began to push me from one building to another. Blocking the path was a school district work truck, positioned right in our way. My dad pushed me in my wheelchair off of the path and into the mud. It was a struggle to get the chair (now covered in mud) back onto the path as it weighed several hundred pounds. He got me to class, then took the chair out in the hall and began the drying process.

After it was all over, he went to the vice principal of the school. He started with, "I don't mean to complain here..." and proceeded to tell the administrator of the situation. The vice principal immediately responded with, "I will have that truck moved, right now!" My dad replied that was kind, but he didn't think that his handicapped son was owed anything. The vice principal replied, "Oh, yes we do owe him something. We owe him the common courtesy and respect that we owe all of our students."

The truck was moved before we saw it again. Do you think that the vice principal would have reacted the same way had my dad gone in yelling and screaming? Or what if he had approached the situation whining and demanding? Maybe...but it wouldn't have shown how a positive person with a positive attitude can handle challenges. His attitude showed how a Christian should deal with life's situations, and I am thankful for the example.

Slip 'n' Slide

One cold winter day when I was in college, we had a small amount of snow fall. Now, unless you live in a southern state, you don't realize how a tiny amount of snow can really shut down a city. People from the north laugh when our schools close for less than an inch of snow, but our city is simply not equipped to handle snow because it falls so infrequently. Well, we had a small amount of snow that day, and many businesses/schools had announced they were closed. Of course, with my lack of luck, Tarrant County College was open and having classes.

So, I bundled up and made my way across campus to my first class. I hit a few patches of ice and had a lot of fun sliding around in my wheelchair. I was one of five students that showed up that morning out of a class of thirty. My World Literature professor held class as usual. I later found out through a college newspaper article about me that he had planned on giving everyone a break that morning until he saw me in class. He decided that if I could make class, then so could every other student in the class. Guess that was the reason for the pop quiz. Oops! ☺

I could have complained...I could have whined...I could have stayed at home that day. But, then, I would have missed out on the quiz. More importantly, whining would have accomplished nothing. I had fun that day just like any other day.

Got it?

Have you caught the lesson yet? Don't whine.

But, it's so much more than that.

Not only should you go through life without the whine, but a positive attitude can accomplish so much more. In other words, don't just cut out the whining, but practice the opposite. Shower people with positive words and show the world a positive attitude. Being positive may get you some things you wouldn't get otherwise, but way beyond that, the power of a positive attitude can do wonders for others around you!

You're Not That Important

My dad and I were recently speaking at one of the largest events that we'd attended. The engagement was not the largest in attendance, but it was one of our first events where we were the "stars of the show" so to speak. We arrived at our hotel, and were greeted by the Executive Director of the foundation that was bringing us in to speak as well as a waiting bellman. We were quickly checked in, taken to our room, and helped with unloading. When we got to our room, we were surprised with a large basket of goodies. Once we unloaded our personal effects, the same bellman walked all of our products and us to the convention area so we could set up. We were the honored guests at the VIP reception where everyone received a copy of our book, <u>All He Needs for Heaven</u> (www.allheneedsforheaven.com), compliments of the organization hosting us. My picture was on the front cover of the program, and many said they felt honored to meet us. We were seated at the head table, given a glowing introduction, and a standing ovation when we finished. Some people waited until long after the event was over just to buy some of our products and to speak to us.

Quite frankly, I enjoyed the way we were treated. I was blown away, and my ego was swelling by the second. Then, my dad reminded me, we have to remember who we are and not let this inflate our egos. Why? Because, in the grand scheme of things, we are not that important. Sure, that evening we were the main attraction, but in life, I have to keep a level head or my perspectives can get out of line quickly.

I'm On My Honeymoon...Leave Me Alone!

Before owning my own travel agency, I worked from home for another agency. Characteristically, self-employed business-people tend to stay attached to their cell-phones, email, etc, no matter where they are. After all, if you aren't working, you aren't bringing in any money. I quickly realized once I got married that I had to set specific working hours so that I didn't try to work all the time and thus, neglect my wife. That's even more important, now, with an infant daughter. When Daddy is done working, it is play time and that shouldn't be interrupted.

I had been with the other agency for several years when Joni and I got married. In planning time away for my honeymoon, I told the owner  and several other agents that I would not be reachable for any reason via email or phone during our trip. Their response was amazement. They could not believe that I would be disconnected from work while on vacation, and they also couldn't believe that I would neglect my clients for an entire week. I told them that this marriage was going to start on the "right foot," and there was no way I would change my mind. So, we had a nice, peaceful honeymoon with no work.

Guess what I learned? I wasn't important enough to the company or my clients for me to work on vacation. They didn't need me for an entire week, and the world didn't come to an end without me. I find peace in the fact that I'm not needed all the time. I need some down time to rest, to enjoy my family, and to recharge for when I am needed. I'm not so important that the world can't function without me, and that's a good feeling.

Like Father, Like Son

I have heard my dad tell of learning this same lesson. In the late 1970s, Dad was preaching at a church in Louisiana, and he and Mom, also, worked with the fourth, fifth, and sixth graders. Once each summer, they would take the fourth, fifth, and sixth graders to Six Flags over Texas. On a Tuesday, they left at 6:00 in the morning and returned at midnight. On Wednesday, the teenagers of the church came to them with a big request. The teens were scheduled to go to Six Flags the next day, Thursday, but their sponsor could not go. Mom and Dad agreed to go back to Six Flags, and this time, they left at 6:00 and returned at 2:00 the next morning. Dad felt like he had rescued the teens.

The second trip to Six Flags complicated an extremely busy week. Dad was to go with the Singles of the church and speak Friday evening at their campout. He and Mom were to begin a week at our Christian camp on Sunday. Dad would be the director, and Mom was to be the banker. As usual, Dad was to preach on Sunday morning.

On Friday, while hurriedly making phone calls about camp, a kidney stone sent him to the hospital. The stone stopped moving, but it was blocking his right ureter. In those days, major, invasive surgery was his only option. He insisted that he get to preach Sunday. (When a stone stops moving, the patient feels no pain.) Still, Dad underwent surgery on Monday, and spent the week in the hospital.

The Singles had a successful campout without a speaker. Dad's assistant director at camp ran the camp week quite capably, and Mom filled in as his assistant. Everything that seemed to depend on Dad's presence and direction was taken care of by someone else. Dad has said that it seemed like the world could not spin without his direction. Obviously, he was not that important.

The Self-Important Driver

You are driving home from work one day and approach a traffic light. You are going the speed limit, and as the light changes to yellow, you make that all important, flash decision.

"Can I beat the red light?"

Don't say you haven't tried it or at least thought it. ☺

Red-light running is on the rise nationwide. In a six-year study, the Insurance Institute for Highway Safety found that deadly crashes at red lights increased at more than three times the rate of all other types of fatal auto accidents.

Why? I know why. The people that run those lights seem to think they are that important. Wherever it is that they are headed, it is so important to not spend an extra minute or two at a red light that they are willing to risk not only their own lives, but the lives of everyone else at that intersection.

If we didn't think so highly of ourselves, maybe we would be happy enough to slow down and spend an extra minute at a red light. Slow down...enjoy life!

We've Got it Without You

Recently, my wife and I had our first child. Hannah Jane was born on March 6th, 2008, and has brought an amazing amount of joy into our lives. Her "belly laugh" can cure the worst grumpy day anyone is having.

Now, at the time of delivery, I was still leading worship every Sunday for the Plymouth Park Church of Christ. I had prepared them with proposed worship orders and backup leaders for several weeks just in case anything prevented us from getting back to normal life so soon after the baby.

The day of delivery came, and while Joni was in labor, Hannah decided she was ready to come out...hands first. This called for a cesarean section because of the danger to her umbilical cord. So, we stayed the requisite five days in the hospital, and were released. Two days after being home, we had to return to the hospital as Joni was very sick. We spent another week there, and after a second operation, all was well again.

While we were spending that second week in the hospital, I attempted to contact the preacher at the congregation where I was serving to make sure all was going well, and to see if my assistance was needed. He simply replied that I had a much more important job to take care of...to tend to my wife. He said, "We've got it without you. Take care of Joni." I am thankful to this day for the support that church showed us, and I am thankful for the lesson I learned. I do like feeling needed, but sometimes, much more important things need to be taken care of, and the world does not spin based on my command.

Stop and Smell the Roses

So, the lesson here? Slow down. Life is too short for us to run through it. Blink, and you'll miss the most important moments. Realize that your family and your God are much more important than you, and in that realization, find peace and happiness.

Adjust Your Priorities:
Invest Yourself in Others

Let's face facts. We live in a "ME" focused society. This can be seen in the vehicle accidents caused by road rage, the rampant purchasing of any new technology, and in those who step on other workers on the way up the never-ending corporate ladder.

In the fall of 2008, we had one of the worst financial problems in the history of this country. At the time of writing these words, the credit crunch is still a problem. Beyond the finger pointing as to who is responsible, we know one thing: Many people borrowed more than they could pay back. We are a society that is focused on wanting the best, and wanting it now. The majority of our country's citizens are focused on one thing… "ME!"

I suggest that this is not only the wrong path to happiness, but it is **a straight and slippery road to a miserable life**. That seems counterintuitive, doesn't it? Common sense would say that if I focused on making myself happy through always getting my way, I would be happy, right?

I truly believe that when we focus on the needs and happiness of others, only then will we be truly happy. How do we focus on others? Change our priorities!

Why Don't You Answer Your Cell Phone?

My wife has teased me ever since we got married about my lack of cell phone usage. I hate cell phones. I think they might as well be shown as the ball & chain that they are. Think about it for a second. Why do you need to be reached 24/7? Some might say for an emergency, and for that reason, I would agree.

But, does your office have your cell phone number? Why do they need to reach you outside of office hours? Do they own you? Up until recently, I never had my cell phone on. As I viewed it, the purpose of my cell phone was in case I needed to call someone in an emergency. Recently, I've been using it for speaking contacts, so it is on, but I don't always answer it.

If you call me after office hours, and I don't recognize the number, I won't answer…for ANY reason.

The way I see it, my priorities are set, and no one can change them but me. I don't mean that to say that you aren't important to me, but rather, you are not as important as my downtime with my family. We have to put limits on outside interruptions when we are with people that matter to us the most.

Focusing on Others Starts at Home

My family and their happiness are more important than my own. I am convinced that more marriages would stay together if we could grasp that point. The Bible commands husbands and wives to be outwardly focused on each other. In *The Message*, a modern-day translation of the Bible, Ephesians 5:21-28 reads:

> "Out of respect for Christ, be courteously reverent to one another.
>
> Wives, understand and support your husbands in ways that show your support for Christ. The husband provides leadership to his wife the way Christ does to his church, not by domineering but by cherishing. So, just as the church submits to Christ as he exercises such leadership, wives should likewise submit to their husbands.

Husbands, go all out in your love for your wives, exactly as Christ did for the church—a love marked by giving, not getting. Christ's love makes the church whole. His words evoke her beauty. Everything he does and says is designed to bring the best out of her, dressing her in dazzling white silk, radiant with holiness. And that is how husbands ought to love their wives."

Do you see how that passage is totally focused on what one spouse ought to do for the other? These are commands to the husband and wife to love and support each other. When we are outwardly focused in our marriages, we fill each other up and allow our marriages to fully blossom. Only by focusing on one another can we be truly happy.

'Tis Better to Give Than to Receive

When my family moved to the Pipeline Road Church of Christ in 1991, I was eleven years old. Pipeline (now called Legacy) had an annual event then called Give Away Day that still continues to this day. Give Away Day is held one Saturday a year, and for months leading up to the event, church members give tons of gently used clothes, furniture, kids' school supplies, toys, etc. Then, volunteers arrange these goods in various places in the church building. When the weekend arrives, people from all over the Dallas/Fort Worth Metroplex come to the church to get things that they need. Each family is taken through the building by a member of the church and **GIVEN** whatever they need. I have heard the event described as "a big department store with no price tags." It is amazing!

I remember the child who came to the food section and exclaimed, "Look, Mommy...FOOD!"

I remember the man whom I led through who only wanted a business suit so that he could present a good image at his job interview the next day. I offered him more, but he told me that many other people who were there that day had a greater need than he did, and he refused to take anything else.

I remember the children I've taken into the toy room, and to see the look on their faces when they realize that any of these toys can be theirs...it wouldn't break Mommy and Daddy's heart to have to tell them, "No" this time.

Give Away Day is incredible, and so many people are blessed. But, what Give Away Day does for the families who get what they need is **NOTHING** compared to what the event does for the spirit of the host church. The event itself takes so much work from hundreds of volunteers. The Sunday after Give Away Day, one might think that the church would be tired from all the work. I'm not saying they aren't physically tired, but in terms of the spirituality and mentality of the church, it is the most "alive" Sunday of the year. The buzz among the church is amazing, and the worship that morning is always awesome.

I am convinced that Give Away Day does more for the Legacy Church of Christ than it does for the community. Maybe that's what God had in mind all along. In Luke 14, Jesus is telling a story about hosting a banquet, and in verses 12-14, he says:

> "When you give a luncheon or dinner, do not invite your friends, your brothers or relatives, or your rich neighbors; if you do, they may invite you back and so you will be repaid. But when you give a banquet, invite the poor, the crippled, the lame, the blind, and **you will be blessed.** Although they cannot repay you, you will be repaid at the resurrection of the righteous."

When we invite those who are never invited, **we receive the blessing.**

"You Changed My Life"

At our speaking engagements, my dad and I always make it a point to be available to our listeners afterwards as we love to get to meet them. People are so inspired by our story that they often like to come to the back and share their own story. I have found that the best way to serve in that situation is to listen. When our story touches someone, the natural response is for them to want to connect with us, and we love it! I did have to get used to one phrase I've heard over and over again, now that we are speaking on a regular basis. The first time I heard this phrase, I was uncomfortable with it.

"You changed my life."

Really? I mean…it's just my story.

"You changed my life."

Really? But who am I that I can change lives?

"You changed my life."

Then…it hit me square between the eyes. This is what God can do through a broken body. Not having arms has not brought a lot of good things to my life in and of itself, but God can turn bad into good. So, when I invest myself into pouring out my story and reliving bad moments along with the good, I give a chance for my listeners to see what God can do. Their response, sometimes, is a changed life. Would I be able to affect lives if I didn't invest myself into others? Are you allowing your priorities to be in line so that you can be used to change lives?

Believe me – No amount of money, things, etc, can make my day brighter than to hear the phrase, "You changed my life." **And, I know it isn't me who's changing lives…so when I hear that phrase, I praise God.**

Serving others is a top priority, and it leads to the happiest moments in life.

How Can Changing My Priorities Lead to Happiness?

Ok, so if I change my priorities, how does that get me closer to happiness? Simple. If I'm not so important, I can better serve others around me. If my wife needs me, I'm not so important as to tell her she has to wait. Aside from God, my family is my top priority.

They come first…way above anyone else…especially my own desires. I committed to that level of priority when I said, "I do."

Throughout every day, both good things and bad seek my attention. I have to choose what gets my attention. If I haven't made that choice at the beginning of the day, then choosing correctly at the end of the day might not be so easy. Very simply put, my level of happiness is directly tied to how well I attend to my true priorities. If I work hard all day long, and then continue to work into the evening, I've failed my family. I may be important to my business, but that won't get me nearly as far in a happy life as being important to my family. We have to choose who and what will get our time in life. To whom are you important? The answer to that question will reveal your priorities. Being important to your office may earn you big promotions and lots of money, but as we discovered earlier, money doesn't bring happiness.

Instead, my advice is to think about the most important people in your life and make an effort to become important to them by serving them. I have a unique view on this because I need help throughout most days in order to make it through the day without arms. In helping me with various things that are difficult or impossible to accomplish without arms, my wife and family show me that I'm important to them. And, in turn, the time and love that I show them shows that they are important to me.

Investing yourself in others is the key to a deflated self-importance and ultimately, to happiness. Making others a priority in your life will make for a happier life, and not only that, you will be able to change others' lives around you!

Giving to others makes the giver feel better than the receiver. Try it! Get out there and volunteer. Find a church to belong to and get to work. Or, simply find a friend in need and give of yourself. You will see amazing changes in yourself when you put yourself out there for others.

9

Use What You Have

Remember "Jane" and her situation way back in Chapter 1? (You can turn back if you need to...don't worry, I'll wait right here.) Her situation was horrible and my heart went out to her, but I also had to keep myself from correcting her. She spent all of her time here on this earth wishing, praying, and hoping that her circumstances would change. Her number one goal in life was for the medical problems plaguing her son to be fixed. Then, once fixed, she felt that she would be able to serve. Fix this first, then serve?

That's backwards!

Serve. And if something were to happen that fixed the situation or made it better, great. But whether or not that happens, you serve. **You use what you have instead of wishing for what you don't have.**

Sometimes, Not Having Arms is a Bonus

The first time I attended a musical at Dallas Summer Musical's Fair Park Music Hall, the house manager was not happy with me. You see, I had neglected to mention when purchasing the tickets that I was in an electric wheelchair. I had been used to parking my wheelchair and walking up stairs if needed to wherever we were sitting…which was usually in the cheap seats. The house manager (head usher) told me that they had special arrangements for people in wheelchairs, and that next time, I was to call a certain person at the box office.

So, I did just that. I was told that Dallas Summer Musicals would be more than happy to pull seats out of the row just in front of the beltline aisle on the orchestra floor. I told the rep that we couldn't afford those seats as they were some of the best in the house. She said that since I could not choose to sit in my wheelchair in the balcony (the building is so old that it doesn't have an elevator), that they thought it only fair to offer these much nicer seats at the same price as the last row in the balcony. WOW! Now, we go to musicals all the time, sit on the orchestra level, and pay a little more than we do to go to a movie theater.

Our favorite place in the whole nation to spend our vacation is the Walt Disney World Resort in Orlando, FL. Disney bends over backwards to provide the necessary accommodations, and there are benefits all over the parks for people in wheelchairs.

Now, I don't say any of this to brag. Far from it. In fact, I've had people accuse me of using my handicap to my advantage. First, I say that my handicap has so many bad things about it, that when good things come my way, I take them. But, beyond that, there are always opportunities that come to you because of what you have. I say, seize the opportunities that come, and don't worry about those that don't. You have to be comfortable with what you have, or you'll never be happy.

You Have to Start Somewhere

When I first began speaking and telling people my story, I didn't want to start at the bottom of the speaking industry. I wanted, just like many others, to not have to work my way up. Why work your way up in this industry?

I was conveying this ambition to my friend, Jeff Walling, who is a pretty big speaker/preacher in the churches of Christ. He smiled and said, "You've got to start somewhere."

You see, I could sit around and wish that I could speak at the biggest gatherings, the biggest venues, and for the biggest companies. And, in the meantime, I would be missing out on a ton of awesome opportunities that are right in front of me.

Sure, these aren't the biggest crowds, but they sure do listen well...

Sure, these aren't the biggest venues, but the crews have been some of the best to work with...

Sure, these aren't the biggest companies, but they are some of the nicest...

Catch the idea? If I hadn't jumped in at the bottom and used what I had, I wouldn't have gotten started at all. Now, I do continue to strive for the best, but I am also content with where my speaking business is, right now.

He'll Use What He Came With

When I was very young, the Shriners Hospital in Shreveport, LA, wanted to fit me with myoelectric arms and leg extensions. I quickly did away with the leg extensions as I could not walk in them, but the arms stuck with me for much longer. I could use them to carry items, play games, etc, and even learned how to control them by sending electrical impulses from my brain instead of moving my muscles. They were impressive machinery back in the 1980s.

...AND I HATED THEM.

They were hot, cumbersome, and had awkward movements. I remember in particular that the wrists on them did not rotate to compensate if I moved the entire arm. So, if I picked up a glass of milk, it spilled all over me long before I could get it to my mouth simply because the arms couldn't do as much as regular human arms could do. Oh, and they were heavy, too, which made for additional pain.

I can remember that I was required to wear them for a certain amount of time every day for practice. My parents and my brother and sister did as much as they could to make practice time fun by playing games with me. Nothing they could do, though, convinced me to like the arms. My feet were so much faster and much more natural to me. I remember very well how I longed for practice time to be over each and every time I had to put them on. And, these had to be pretty strong feelings because I remember them vividly...and I was only three years old!

We took many trips to see a limb deficiency specialist in Atlanta, GA, by the name of Dr. Richard King. At the time, he was the country's foremost specialist in the field of my handicap, and I can remember many trips to see him. I just thought it was such a treat to get to go on an airplane. I even remember eating pancakes on a plane one morning when I was young, on our way to see Dr. King. (That was back when riding on a plane was a luxury instead of a hassle. But, that's a completely different book!)

One particular visit to Dr. King proved very beneficial to me and my desire to not use my myoelectric arms. I was playing in a patient room on the floor while my parents talked to Dr. King. They were raving about all the progress I had made with my arms, and how proud they were of me. I had made tons of progress and could use the artificial arms quite well. So, Dr. King asked my parents to put the arms on me so that he could evaluate me. My dad tells me that they had the arms on me for about a minute before Dr. King announced, "Take those off of him, put them in a closet, and never make him wear them again!"

My parents were stunned. First of all, these arms weren't cheap. Because they had been donated to us by the Shriners, my parents felt a sense of obligation due to their cost. Second, my parents saw such potential in what those arms could do for me in the future. Luckily for my future happiness, Dr. King saw something else. He told my parents that I had rejected the arms. "What?" they said, "He's only three years old. How can he reject anything?"

The doctor told them that while I had not outwardly refused to wear them, he knew that I had rejected them by how I reacted once they were on me. He told my parents, "Chet 'shut down' once the arms were on him." He said that I was happy and playing while the arms were off, and as soon as they were on, my shoulders slumped, my smile went away, and I stopped playing. Then, he said the now-famous line in our family: "If you keep making him wear these, he'll go on TV some day and amaze the nation. Then, he'll go backstage, take them off, and use what he came with!"

I LOVE the line. "Use what he came with." What I am about to say is not to be taken as a slam against my parents. They tried their best to do what was right for me, and many doctors had suggested the myoelectric arms. But, for my WHOLE life, people have tried to make me look like everyone else. I have had artificial arms and legs...I have had some clothes that were meant to hide my lack of limbs...I even had a doctor once that wanted to do surgery on one of my ankles because I don't walk like everyone else does.

Doctors have been notorious in my life for wanting to figure out my insides. Now, don't get me wrong, I've had some great doctors, and I've finally found one that wants to treat my various routine sicknesses when I go see him as opposed to wanting to poke and prod to see how my bones are structured.

Can you imagine going to the doctor with a runny nose and instead of him listening to your symptoms and doing something to make you better, he chooses to lie you down and theorize on how you walk? "Ridiculous!" you might say. But, I don't have to imagine...it has actually happened to me. One doctor wanted to shoot dye in me to see how my kidneys worked. I said that I didn't have problems with my kidneys. He said he needed to know, just in case. Yeah...right...put him off my list of people I never want to see again.

Why do all these doctors want to change me? I think that people without handicaps have a drive to "fix" those of us who do. I don't think they have bad intentions, in fact, just the opposite. They see their "fixing" as beneficial.

Listen. I do it my way. I use what I came with. And, I'm HAPPY by doing so.

I am so grateful to Dr. King, and to my parents, for allowing me to be who I am instead of someone who pretends to be different just to make things easier on those around me. It may have scared my parents at times, especially those times I went snow skiing as seen above, but I truly appreciate being allowed to be "me."

I've said it before, and I'll say it again. I would change nothing about the way I look. (Ok, maybe I could lose a few pounds, but you get the idea.)

Maybe I need to be blunt. If I were offered arms, and I mean genuine, real human arms (not artificial ones), I wouldn't take them.

I am totally happy and comfortable in my body. I use what I have to the glory of God, and I don't wish or pray for things to be different. And, with that attitude, I've been able to do and see amazing things in my life. That attitude has allowed me to live a happy life.

I don't pretend that happiness comes easily, though. So, what's the one way to achieve happiness?

10

Happiness is a Choice

Okay. Revolutionary moment. As my friend, Jeff Walling, is fond of saying this will "crack your taco." This one phrase will change your life if you let it. Ready?

You have to CHOOSE happiness.

Sorry if the simplicity of the statement was a let-down, but the phrase's power is in its simplicity. All you have to do to achieve happiness in life is to choose it. Seriously. There's no secret formula…no elusive "thing" you have to buy. In fact, even though I've shown you multiple avenues to take to achieve greater happiness, they mean nothing if you do not make the choice. Happiness is all in your attitude. If you make a daily choice to be happy, you will be.

Everyone Fails My Class

In my first year in college, I met a professor that really changed my outlook on life. And…she wasn't even a good professor. In fact, I would have to say that this particular professor was the worst "teacher" I encountered in my entire collegiate career.

She taught College Algebra, and I needed to take the course in order to fulfill a math credit. Now, let me veer off for a moment from the story to tell you that math has always been easy for me. I loved all math-related subjects, and numbers have always been easy for me to pick up on. So, College Algebra was not really a challenge for me.

On the first day of class, the professor stood up in front of the class and announced the following:

> "50% of the students who take this class either fail the course or drop out before the semester is done. If you think you will be one of those students, you should drop now to save yourself the trouble."

I could write an entire book on all of the ways her opening day speech was wrong. She set up a negative expectation from day one, and of course, her speech had a negative effect on the class. Shoulders slumped, eyes looked toward the ground, and one student even got up to leave. Obviously, the power-trip of being a know-it-all had gone to the professor's head long ago, and she was only a "professor" by title, not by called profession. She had none of the qualities of a good teacher, and I believe she chose the wrong business. Teaching is about helping others, not demeaning them. I determined from that moment to make a difference in the class. I **chose** to have a positive attitude and to be happy in the face of this problem.

So, fast forward about two weeks. The day of the first chapter exam had come, and that morning I happened to find myself riding the elevator with the professor. After just a moment of silence, she very smugly asked, "Are you ready for **my** test?"

Now, in case you don't know me, I would like to share with you a condition I have. I believe it is commonly referred to as "foot-in-mouth syndrome." I say things before my brain can stop me. So, in the same exact smug tone, I replied, "I was born ready." Thankfully, at that moment, the elevator doors opened and I did not give her a chance to spew any more of her negativity.

The professor began the test with the SAME speech.

> "Over 50% of the students who take my class fail or drop out. If you think that could be you, leave before you take this test so that you can drop rather than fail."

UGH! What garbage! I was even more determined to "fix her."

I was the first student to finish the test, and I wheeled up to the front of the room to turn it in. The professor, in a rather loud voice, asked, "Well, how do you think you did?" The entire class looked up from their tests to see my answer, and I realized that they needed a confidence boost. So, I grinned, and while looking at my classmates, I replied, "I got a 100% on **YOUR** test." Several classmates smiled back, and the professor simply grunted. I wheeled out of the room with a big smile on my face trying to figure out what kind of situation I had just created.

At the end of the next class period, the professor began to hand back the test. You could have cut the tension in the room it was so thick. She walked up to me first, and as she handed back my test, she announced, "You did make a 100." There was not a smile on her face. In fact, I got the distinct impression that she was upset that I had bested her "monster" test. She handed back the rest of the exams in silence and left the room.

As soon as she left the room, I stood up and said,

> "Hey, you guys, math comes easy for me and it's obvious that she is not going to *teach* us this semester. Can we form a big study group to make sure that no one fails this semester?"

Can you guess what happened? Not only did my offer lift the spirits of everyone else in the room, but at the end of the semester, NOT ONE STUDENT FAILED. In fact, everyone passed with a high C-average or above. Several students thanked me for actually being the teacher that semester. In fact, several of them had taken her course more than once, and this time, they finally passed.

Why? I believe it is because my positive attitude gave them the confidence they needed. Sure, I'm okay with saying that what we studied in our study group helped, but much more than that, they finally had a voice telling them, "You can do it!" The attitude during class time also changed after our study group was formed. Would you believe that we started to have fun in math class? Not only that, but at the end of the semester, the professor said she couldn't have been prouder of this class. She was actually taking pride in our success. So, maybe our positive attitude helped her, too!

I don't tell this story to show how good I was, or how gracious I was to form a study group to help others. I tell it to show how a choice to make a difference through happiness and confidence changed an entire classroom one semester.

What's Your Choice?

I end every talk I give with the same illustration, and it is only fitting for me to close this book in the same way.

I have two sides of the bed that I can choose to wake up on each and every day. On one side, I allow all of the negative things about life to consume my attitude. I choose to be a negative, broken person.

And, let's be bluntly honest here…if anyone has the "right" to choose this side, I do. Life has dealt me a very cruel hand, and I believe that society would not judge me poorly if I did choose the negative side. After all, others with disabilities have entire lives full of pity parties, and many times, their family members, friends, and society all become enablers of their poor attitude.

So, life's been unfair to me…is it my right to choose a negative attitude towards life?

Absolutely not! My life is not determined by my circumstances, rather by my attitude in the face of my circumstances. The negative side of life gets me nowhere. Not only would my family and friends have to put up with a poor attitude, but God is not praised by a negative life.

Let me say that, again:
God is NOT praised by a negative life.

I believe that we are on Earth to show others the grace and love of God, and I cannot show that in my life with a negative attitude. Not one person has ever walked up to a self-pitying Christian and asked them about Jesus. God is not reflected in negativity...and if I am made in His image (Genesis 1:26-27), I have no choice but to reflect His grace and love for all mankind.

So, the only choice I have each morning, (and the only choice you can make if you want to live a happy life) is to get up, put a smile on your face, know that God is in control, and that He loves you. Being secure in the sovereignty of God and in His love will prepare you for whatever life throws your way. God is my refuge and my strength, and without Him, I would not be able to face a life without arms. But with Him, I know that I can face anything...even life without arms.

You see, we live in a fallen world. A world that is separated from its Creator is by definition, broken. But, because of God's love for us, He sent His son to die for our sins. And in that sacrifice and in Jesus' resurrection from the grave, we are made whole.

So, am I broken because I don't have arms? In the world's eyes, I suppose so. But, in God's eyes, I am a whole person whom He loves so much that He gave His own son as a sacrifice so that I could one day live with Him. God loves every person on this planet in that same way. Our brokenness is made whole through God whether or not we have the perfect set of circumstances in life.

I don't have arms, but I'm whole.

Maybe you have cancer, but you're whole.

Maybe you are about to lose your job. You're still whole.

Maybe your home life is a wreck. You're still whole.

You see, the world sees me as un-whole, but God sees me as His child. He sees everyone that way. So, no matter what your situation, you can CHOOSE to live a happy life. Because...

I'm not broken...and neither are you.